This devotion is something that I have dreamed and longed to create, but everything is in God's timing. I want to say thank you to Him first and foremost for being the faithful God that He is and speaking dreams over my heart and being faithful to His word to see them come to fruition.

To my family who was with me through the writing process, literally. To write during home order and a time in history that will be remembered was no easy task, but their presence and encouragement made it possible for this to come to be. Thank you for the love, support (and hours of editing Mom), Mom, Dad, and Peter. Thank you for being my strongest support and your commitment to pouring into me and the dreams God has placed on my heart. I could not have done this without each one of you. I love you deeply and thank God that I get to live out my dreams with my family by my side, I wouldn't want to share my dreams becoming a reality without you all!

To Josh, for the countless hours of prayer, speaking the truth, and pushing me to complete this project. For all the times I wanted to give up, thank you for being my loudest supporter, strongest advocate, and dedication to seeing my dreams becoming a reality.

To my friends who read the first draft, gave me feedback, and believed in this dream as it was coming to be, thank you for your support, kind words, and constant cheerleading during this project.

This devotional took over a year to write, edit, produce, and I am sure in a couple of years, I will look back and want to change things, but we all have to start somewhere.

Stay surrendered to God's promises and He will remain faithful to His word.

Introduction

When I first read through this psalm, it was during the 2020 COVID-19 global pandemic, and I was exhausted. I had been doing ministry in a whole new way, during completely new circumstances that were really difficult, and I felt completely worn out as though I could barely keep my head above water. However, as I read this psalm, it was like the Lord was whispering truths into the very deepest parts of my heart. He was telling me that though this time was new and things were uncertain, when we are faithful in times of uncertainty, He will bring about a harvest that is different and better than expected. I hope and pray the same for you as you read this.

When the LORD restored the fortunes of Zion, we were like those who dreamed.

- Psalm 126:1

Day 1
Devotional

Dreaming can be scary.

What if we dream, but they don't come true?

Dreaming can also be fun. When was the last time you dreamed so much and so big that your stomach got butterflies out of anticipation and excitement? You knew that the work would be difficult, but it would be more worth it than you ever knew was possible?

Something to note though.

This verse doesn't start out with dreaming; it starts with,

"When the Lord restored..."

In order for something to be restored,

it first has to be broken or at least not working the way it was intended.

Oftentimes, we tend to think that we can completely forget/ignore things that have happened in the past: hurts, rejection, missed opportunities, dreams, but that's not necessarily how God works.

Have you ever seen Kintsugi pottery?

It is a style of Japanese pottery in which the broken pieces from the original are fused back together using different elements (gold, silver, platinum).

Something new and even more beautiful than the original is then formed.

As I read this verse, the picture of this kind of pottery came to mind.

"When the Lord restored..."

The Lord is in the business of restoring,

but often we are so busy looking at the broken pieces,

that we miss the restoration process and

even miss the more beautiful result that He is creating.

Sometimes, in order to dream, we first have to be restored.

I don't know about you, but I don't want to miss out on dreaming God-sized dreams because I didn't let God take my broken pieces and make something more beautiful.

Application

What do you need to let the Lord restore?

What parts of your heart and
story do you feel the Lord asking you to give to Him to restore,
so He can show you how to dream again?

Takeaway

Maybe you already know how to let the Lord restore,
but you are having trouble trusting Him to let you dream again.

Ask Him to help you dream; ask Him to show you how to dream.

There is no one who is more perfect or safer to dream with than God.

Notes

There is no one better

or safer to dream with

than God

Our mouths were filled with

laughter,

our tongues with songs of joy.

Then it was said among the

nations,

the LORD has done great

things for them.

- Psalm 126:2

Day 2
Devotional

Storytelling is powerful.

Have you ever watched a movie during which you had to pace, hide your face, or literally sit on the edge of your seat?

Or have you ever stayed up way too late to finish a book because you couldn't help not knowing what was going to happen next with the characters? Yeah, same.

When I get a new book by Robin Jones Gunn, everyone in my life knows they won't see me for 2 days because once I start it, I won't be able to stop. I am always completely enthralled with the story and have to find out what is going to happen.

However, this is also true of books I have already read. For instance, every Christmas I read the same 3 books: (again by Robin Jones Gunn, can you tell I am a fan?) *Finding Father Christmas*, *Engaging Father Christmas,* and *Kissing Father Christmas*. I could tell you these stories backward and forwards and have had some sweet holiday memories with each book. However, I reread them every year to remind my head and heart about those memories and to just enjoy some of my favorite books.

Do you have practices or traditions you repeat every year?

I often do things like these without even thinking about it, but when it comes to doing this with the Lord, I forget.

I know, I should be saying this is WHAT I do with the Lord, but instead, I thought I would be honest and tell you that I don't do this with him as routinely as I should.

I think this is why I like this part of the verse so much. It reminds me that when we are in seasons or moments of joy and laughter to remember the God who enabled those moments. Enjoy them; share them with others. He wants you to have joy in this life!

Not only that, but to choose to often remind yourself of these joy-filled moments with Him.

The thing about storytelling is that it not only affects the person telling the story, it also affects those who hear the retelling as well.

We can tell and retell so many stories about how the Lord has been faithful in our lives and remind not only ourselves but also others of His faithfulness during difficult times.

Application

What story do you need to tell yourself or someone else today?

What story could you write down, record,
or share with someone about how the Lord
has been faithful during a season of difficulty?

Takeaway

For you, you may be the friend telling the story,
or you may be the one who needs to be reminded of a story of God's faithfulness.

Whichever one you may be, reach out to someone today
and give God some glory by telling a story of His faithfulness.

Storytelling is powerful. What story will you tell today?

Notes

Storytelling

is

powerful

The Lord has done great

things for us,

and we are filled with joy.

- Psalm 126:3

Day 3
Devotional

Laughter and joy are some of the best weapons against our enemy.

I remember when I was in college, and I was having a really tough week, not just with all the tests and stress that are normal in college, but all of that plus a lot of spiritual attacks.

I was sitting on the floor of my room talking with my friend and saying:
"I just can't wait until I get to have a break from fighting all of this."
To which she responded: "Laughter is a great weapon against the enemy."
I looked at her confused. I asked her: "How?"

She said: "It really confuses our enemy. It makes absolutely no sense to him.
When we are able to place the hard life stuff in the
hands of God and then enjoy the day God has given us and the people around us in the middle of the mess, it really disarms our enemy."

To this day, I have never forgotten that conversation.
The exact words are a bit blurred, but I have never forgotten the fact that
laughter is a strong weapon against the enemy. Joy completely disarms our enemy because it doesn't make sense.

It doesn't make sense for us to experience community and growth
while we may also have relationships that are broken and falling apart.

It doesn't make sense when we laugh while storytelling
or are silly with friends while tragedies are happening around us.

It doesn't make sense when we stop and take a pause
in our day to play a game or go for a walk.

It doesn't make sense when we laugh so hard with friends that our sides hurt
when just days or hours before, our faces were stained with tears.
It doesn't make sense.

When we choose to live in joy and have laughter even when life around us is too much,
it not only confuses our enemy, it renders him powerless.
Not only does it not make sense to our enemy;
it doesn't make sense to the world around us.

When we choose joy and laughter even amidst life's difficulties and ever-changing circumstances, we look odd to the rest of the world.

When we choose to believe that God is as great as he claims to be and truly live our lives with joy and laughter, we show those around us that there is a different way to do life.

We show that our God is big enough to hold our lives and give us a break. It shows that we believe: "God will fight for us, we need only be still." (Exodus 14:14)

Application

How can you confuse the enemy today?

Whether or not you are going through a really rough time or just need a joy and laughter break today, choose to let God hold the circumstances and to-do lists and just enjoy sharing life with Him and others.

How can you choose to use laughter and
joy as a weapon of confusion and disarm the enemy?
Play cards (a personal favorite)
Call a friend
See a friend

Takeaway

Whatever it is that will bring you laughter and joy, do it today. Completely confuse the enemy and astound those around you, and maybe even yourself, by letting God hold what is causing you stress and just enjoy the people and the day He has set in front of you.

<u>Notes</u>

Laughter and joy
are some of the best
weapons
against our enemy.

Restore our fortunes, LORD,

like streams in Negev.

- Psalm 126:4

Day 4
Devotional

Have you ever heard a child ask something of their parent?

It isn't a polite: "Excuse me mom/dad, may I please, when it isn't too much trouble, could you please pass me the snack because I am starting to get hungry?"

No kid talks like that. They say: "Snack, please," or just: "Snack, mom?"

They don't use big or fancy words; they just say what they need.

A child states their need to their parent and EXPECTS them to come through.
A child knows that their parent is going to pass them the snack
because they have in the past, and so they believe they will again.

Too often, I know at least for me, I wait to ask God something.

I feel like I need to be in a specific mood and headspace so that I can communicate my thoughts just so, because if I don't ask them in just the right order, then I will misstep or misspeak and get something I don't want.

Other times, I will create a very succinct, but holy prayer,
so that God knows I am here and revering Him,
all the while thinking: "I got places to be."

Any of this sound familiar?

The way we interact with our earthly father is a pretty good indicator of how we interact with God. However, we may not know how to interact with God because of a lack of presence of our earthly father, but it is something we can learn.

When we consider our imperfect, earthly, fatherly examples and how they behave,
we can think that God operates in the same way.

He doesn't, though.

When you look at David and His prayer to the Lord,
David doesn't say "if",
and he doesn't put a caveat on his request before the LORD.

He just states his request.

No ifs, ands, or buts. He just puts his heart out there and asks the LORD to come through,
and because he knows that God has come through in the past,

David believes in the promises of God and knows that He will continue to be faithful
to His promises, both in the current season and in the future.

Application

How are you when it comes to praying to God? Are you completely vulnerable and authentic 100% of the time? Do you come before the throne of grace no matter your head and heart condition because you have grasped that there is nothing that God loves more than His kids?

Whichever one of the prompts written above is easy for you, thank God for it. Whichever of these is difficult, take it to the throne room of heaven right now.

Ask God. No matter your to-do list, no matter how you think you ought to approach His throne, just approach it.

Takeaway

God wants you in His throne room. He wants to hear your voice.

Notes

God wants to hear

your requests,

all of them.

Those who sow with tears

will reap with songs of joy

- Psalm 126:5

Day 5
Devotional

Have you ever been through something that you just prayed would end?
What storm in your life have you just cried out for God to put an end to?

I have cried for myself and those around me. I have. I have wept and desired to see God remove us from the terrible time of distance during the COVID-19 homebound order.

This verse is not merely encouraging.
It contains life and truth in the form of a promise
we can take straight to the throne room in heaven.

But you know what is so key about it?

It says: "Those who sow..." The sower has to carry the seed.

There is a choice to be made.

Even if the sower is crying, they still go to the harvest field.

In order to yield a harvest, one must first decide to pick up the seed
and carry it to the field even when it is painful and hard.
We can all walk into the harvest field and ask God to do a miracle, but oftentimes, God wants to use us in partnership to see a harvest created.

The result of continuing to sow during difficult times is given right there in the verse,
"...reap with songs of joy."

Not only does the verse promise that there will be reaping and a harvest will be produced, which should be plenty to keep us still carrying seed to the soil, but because God is so good and so kind, it will happen with joy.

Now the Hebrew word for joy in this verse is the word: בְּרִנָּה rinnâh, which means gladness, joy, proclamation, and triumph, shouting and singing (studylight.org)

It can seem as though God isn't doing anything.
Perhaps, He is waiting on us until we continue to go to the field
and plant the seeds we have been clutching.
Until we open our palms and let the seeds fall into the soil,
God can't do what only He can do.

We have to stay faithful to our part of the equation:
the showing up, the work, the continuing on even when it is through tears.

Showing up looks different for everyone, and every circumstance is different, so don't compare how you are walking to your field with the seeds in your hand to the person next to you. That is a sure way to trip and fall and distract you from getting to your field.

Application

As you take a look at your day and your life,
what is the field God has asked you to carry seed to? How's that going?

Do you know what your field is? If not, take some time today and ask the Lord and then sit in silence and see if He gives you a tugging on your heart.

Oftentimes, God has placed a field in front of us, but we see it so often that we don't even recognize it as a place to sow seeds: your workplace, your roommates, your family, your friends, your social media, your dating life, your lack of dating life, your church, your city.

These are just a couple of examples of
possible fields the Lord is placing on your heart.

How can you sow during this time of uncertainty?
Commit to more time with the Lord?
Commit to being more consistent in your relationships?
Commit to being more present?
Commit to investing in others even if you don't know if they will invest in return?

Takeaway

Sowing seeds looks different for everyone, but it doesn't have to be complicated.
Take the complications and excuses out of it.

Call one person today that you can schedule a life conversation with. Sow a seed into someone else, and as you do, I will be praying that you will reap with joy…and soon!

<u>Notes</u>

Showing up

looks different

for everyone

Those who go out weeping,

carrying seed to sow,

will return with songs of joy,

carrying sheaves with them.

- Psalm 126:6

Day 6
Devotional

I am NOT a runner.

Seriously, for a little bit in high school, I ran, but that was just to impress a boy (honesty, am I right?) and then I went on jogs in college. My jam is the gym. So, when a worldwide pandemic took away my option to go to the gym, I started running again. I made it a goal to run/jog/walk a minimum of 2 miles, 5-6 times a week. Let me tell you, it hurt when I first started. I would come home, and be in pain and have to stretch. However, one day, I was running, and I kept thinking: "I want to go a little farther. I want to go a little farther," and you know what? I did! I went farther than I ever had! I ran over 4 miles and walked another 2.

Oftentimes, when we are walking through a difficult time,
it can feel like we are not making any progress.
We keep showing up to work, showing up for our families,
communities, financial responsibilities, and it can be difficult.

Have you ever worked really hard at something,
to the point that you are crying on your floor or so angry and frustrated
because you don't see results, and you feel like you aren't getting anywhere?

Yeah, we have all felt that.
We have felt and experienced the
"what is the point?"
of this life and its difficulties.

However, the thing I love about this verse is the fact that it paints an amazing picture
of what it looks like to be faithful even when it is gut-punching hard.

It promises that those who go out,
even if they are weeping while they are carrying seed to sow,
they will RETURN WITH JOY!!

They don't let their circumstances dictate their faithfulness.
They let their faithfulness dictate how they respond to their circumstances.

They carry the seed, knowing what God can do.
They carry the promise of belief into the field even when it hurts.

And you know what? It says they returned with songs of joy, carrying sheaves.

They yielded a harvest.

They came back with a result.

They saw the fruit of the work they put in even when it cost them their comfort and tears.

Application

If you are in the process of carrying seed to sow even though it is difficult and even though it seems easier to just let the seed fall, I am right beside you, friend. Keep showing up, even today, a day at a time, and remember to breathe through the pain.

Take some time today to put on worship, and ask the Lord to help you carry that seed to the field. Not only will He listen; He wants to do it with you.

Takeaway

You are not alone.

Keep walking, breathing and holding the hand that was pierced for you on the cross.

You are not alone.

Notes

Those who are faithful don't let their circumstances dictate their faithfulness, they let their faithfulness dictate how they respond to their circumstances.

When the LORD restored the fortunes of Zion,
we were like those who dreamed.
Our mouths were filled with laughter,
our tongues with songs of joy.
Then it was said among the nations,
"The LORD has done great things for them."
The Lord has done great things for us,
and we are filled with joy.
Restore our fortunes, LORD,
like streams in the Negev.
Those who sow with tears
will reap with songs of joy.
Those who go out weeping,
carrying seed to sow,
will return with songs of joy,
carrying sheaves with them.

- Psalm 126

Day 7
Devotional

As you wrap up this week of study on God's faithfulness,
I hope you have felt encouraged and have seen God work during this time.

I hope and pray that these are not merely words that you have read on a page,
but that the Lord has used them and spoken to you through them.

One thing is for certain.

What the Lord told me to share with you is just scratching the surface
of the promises of God that can be found in the Bible
and in this specific passage alone.

God's word is multi-layered.

You may read this today, and then a couple of months from now,
reread it and get something completely new.

In fact, I hope you do!

"All scripture is God-breathed
and is useful for teaching, rebuking, correcting
and training in righteousness,
so that the servant of God may be
thoroughly equipped for every good work."
(2 Timothy 3:16-17)

Truth is Truth.

It never loses its potency.

We have to keep seeking,
searching, and listening.
I pray the Holy Spirit has
and continues to whisper truths to you
about this passage.

Live life like you are covered in grace, friend, because you are.

Live life like you

are covered in grace,

because you are.

About the author

Jessica is a multi-passionate, entrepreneur who lives in Kansas City. She is a blogger and has a heart for social media to be a place where God moves and connects people to each other. She longs to be a light in this world and for people to know, understand, and believe that their worth is completely fixed: that nothing they do or don't do can make God love them any more or any less. She has worked for a ministry to millennials in the Kansas City area for 3 years now while completing her Master's degree in Applied Family Sciences. Jessica loves those in her life fiercely. Currently, she is growing her writing platform and developing more devotionals and online courses for people to have healthier and stronger relationships with themselves and others.

A note from Jessica: "Know that you have been prayed for! Yes, you, who picked up, looked at, ordered this book. I have been praying for you and hope that God has used this in your life. More importantly, I hope that you have encountered God in the pages of this devotional. Live in the confidence that God will come through on His promises."

Want more from Jessica?
Check out her info below and connect
with her on social media

JESSICA GRACE CREATIVE LLC
JESSICAGRACETHOMPSON.COM
SOCIAL MEDIA /MARKETING /WRITER
B.S. FAMILY STUDIES AND HUMAN SERVICES
INSTAGRAM/FACEBOOK: JESSICAGRACETHOMPSON

Printed in Great Britain
by Amazon

47983826R00021